Thomas Mann

1875-1955

Seinem ausgezeichneten Porträtisten
Herrn Hermann Berg
München den 23. XII. 29
Thomas Mann

Thomas Mann

1875-1955

Stanley Corngold
Victor Lange
Theodore Ziolkowski

PRINCETON UNIVERSITY LIBRARY
PRINCETON, NEW JERSEY

1975

COPYRIGHT © 1975 BY PRINCETON UNIVERSITY LIBRARY
DESIGNED BY BRUCE D. CAMPBELL
PRINTED IN THE UNITED STATES OF AMERICA
BY PRINCETON UNIVERSITY PRESS AT PRINCETON, NEW JERSEY
ISBN NO. 0-87811-021-6

Table of Contents

Preface	vii
Thomas Mann the Novelist VICTOR LANGE	1
Thomas Mann and the German Philosophical Tradition: Two Essays on Nietzsche STANLEY CORNGOLD	9
Thomas Mann as a Critic of Germany THEODORE ZIOLKOWSKI	17
Thomas Mann and the Emigré Intellectuals THEODORE ZIOLKOWSKI	24
Thomas Mann in Exile VICTOR LANGE	39
The Mann Family STANLEY CORNGOLD	46

Preface

When Thomas Mann paid his first visit to the United States in May 1934, he was already living in exile in Switzerland, but he could hardly have imagined eventual residence in this country. Yet exactly four years later he and his wife entered the United States from Canada on a Czech passport and a permanent residence visa. Germany had annexed Austria in March of that year (Mann was here on an extensive lecture tour at the time), and it is possible he decided then that the deterioration of the political climate did not make even Zurich a safe harbor for enemies of the Third Reich. In any event, he accepted President Harold W. Dodds' invitation to come to Princeton as a lecturer in the Department of Modern Languages and give a number of seminars for students as well as a series of public lectures. In October 1938 he settled down at 65 Stockton Street to begin a new life. In this house he wrote his Goethe-novel, published in Stockholm as *Lotte in Weimar*, in New York as *The Beloved Returns*. Here also he began another major work, *Joseph the Provider*, and that "Maya grotesque," as he called his novella *The Transposed Heads*. For this reason alone it is fitting that Princeton University Library should celebrate the Mann centenary by opening a major exhibition in October 1975.

But another and equally compelling reason is the deep affection a Princeton benefactor, the late Miss Caroline Newton, held for the whole Mann family. The essays in this volume are dedicated to her memory. They were intended to be presented at what would have been her third Thomas Mann Commemoration at Princeton University. The first was held in October 1964 and included the unveiling of the tablet marking his Princeton residence and a Library exhibition entitled "The Literary Career of Thomas Mann." Four years later she helped to organize a second commemoration. The daughter of the bibliophile A. Edward Newton, she was a passionate collector in her own right, and Princeton University Library is the richer for her generous gifts over the years of Thomas Mann letters, manuscripts, first editions, presentation copies, and journals. Since she had a complete command of the German language, she had begun reading Mann while living in Vienna after World War I. In 1929 she met him for the first time, through her friend Jakob Wassermann, in Berlin. When, in 1938, the Manns emigrated, Miss Newton offered them her summer home in Jamestown, Rhode Island "for the duration of the Nazi madness." Thus began a correspondence which lasted seventeen years and a friendship that grew to include Katia Mann and all the children. She said it was three years after Mann's death before she was able to read his letters again. When she published them privately in 1971, she recalled with pride that "the first house in the United States in which Katia and Thomas Mann lived was mine." We hope that the 1975 exhibition of her Mann Collection would also have filled Miss Newton with satisfaction and pride.

Professors Corngold, Lange, and Ziolkowski of the Department of Germanic Languages and Literatures in Princeton University have collaborated on this book and Professor Corngold has been of invaluable aid in preparing the centenary exhibition. On behalf of the Library, I wish to thank them for their wise counsel and kind assistance.

RICHARD M. LUDWIG

Assistant University Librarian for Rare Books and Special Collections

Thomas Mann the Novelist

VICTOR LANGE

Within the varied canon of work which makes Thomas Mann one of the most distinguished and prolific European men of letters, the achievements of the novelist are the most striking and fascinating. Neither the constant demands made upon him as a public figure nor the astonishing burden of a vast correspondence diminished his constant preoccupation with the writing of fiction; it is as the author of a number of masterly short stories and of more than half a dozen spectacular novels that he has made a lasting contribution to the literature of the twentieth century.

Mann was essentially a moralist in the tradition of European humanism, conservative by conviction, fastidious and exacting in his taste, and with strong pedagogical and rhetorical talents. He brought extraordinary narrative gifts, the detachment of an ironic or humorous observer, and a superb sense of style in language to the novel of ideas and to the kind of psychological portraiture which were developed by the masters of nineteenth-century fiction in England, France and Russia. He drew upon a peculiarly German tradition of poetical and lyrical story-telling, and offered fresh formal resolutions to the challenges of an increasingly complex contemporary sensibility.

Yet, his first novel, *Buddenbrooks* (1901), rich in detail and figuration and sustained by a steady, slowly unfolding epic perception, was in design and style a thoroughly original work; no recent European fiction could have served Mann as anything like a usable model: he had read neither Conrad nor Henry James, both later admired for their sustained narrative voice. There was no German tradition of a panoramic novel, and only one contemporary German writer of an unmistakable and congenial tone, Theodor Fontane, had offered in his novels about Prussian life a comparable texture. In *Buddenbrooks* Mann tells the story of a declining family whose effectiveness and public esteem are fatally undermined by the corroding impact of modern philosophical pessimism upon successive generations, and their growing fascination with music and art. It is a work of remarkable maturity which contains, in essence, nearly all the themes, motifs and narrative devices which Mann develops in his subsequent work: Schopenhauer and Nietzsche have determined his experience of the paradoxical counterplay of the normal and the sophisticated, of health and the iridescent reflections of disease and decadence, of representative public ritual and the isolating intensity of feeling.

Mann was not quite prepared for the success which this long novel almost instantly attained: a book, he writes a year after its publication, "which treats the problem of decadence with a sort of humorous hopelessness, cannot be enjoyed, let alone understood, by the public at large." The compelling presence of a story teller and the strategic skill of embodying social and philosophical issues in concretely envisaged figures were even then central ingredients in Mann's artistry. That talent was still more impressively marshalled in the two shorter narratives that have become classic examples of Mann's craftsmanship, in *Tonio Kröger* (1903) and *Death in Venice* (1912).

These two novellas reiterate the theme of the paradoxical relationship between life and insight in the more concentrated perspective of a single figure: the impact of perception upon consciousness produces in *Tonio Kröger* a sense of isolation or alienation which, if it is reflected and rendered palpable in the artist's work, may well be the ineluctable condition of the life of the mind. When the quest for perception is, as in *Death in Venice*, pursued beyond the safeguards of discipline and formal restraint, it inevitably leads to the surrender of life to the demands of truth and beauty: death is the price of radical insight. In these two incomparably elegant stories, Mann states his antithetical patterns of bourgeois and artist, of health and disease, of action and reflection, of community and isolation, in compositions of remarkably pointed symbolic resonance.

Royal Highness (1909) seems a more casual work, a "comedy in the form of a novel"; yet it too offers sets of variations on Mann's theme of the artist's paradoxical commitment to life as well as the formal restraints that threaten to paralyze it. By convention and upbringing, a princely highness is compelled to lead a ceremonial existence, a sham life in which the public performance is applauded as a decorative ritual exercise. By his encounter with a delightful, warm-hearted, and rich girl, Imma Spoelmann, he learns to transcend his life of dutiful representation in love and community. It is a fairy tale in which the conflict between public decorum and private feeling is an allegorical transliteration of the tensions within the artist, between the immediacy of experience and the inescapable restraints of form and order. Here, as in all of Thomas Mann's novels, autobiographical elements and meticulously observed and reported features of contemporary life are transformed in a fictional context.

They become the telling material of *The Magic Mountain* (1924), a novel of ideas planned as a humorous pendant to *Death in Venice* but soon grown to a work of characteristic intricacy and of demanding philosophical scope. A young "nondescript" German engineer visits his ailing cousin in a Swiss sanatorium and there, free of the normal obligations and restraints of life "in the lowlands," is exposed to the pressures of various attitudes and convictions. Inescapably drawn into the rhythm of life and death, day and night, health and disease, waking and dreaming, musical transcendence and medical diagnosis, all of these soon felt and understood as inescapable polarities, Hans Castorp gradually gains an intense sense of self as well as a heightened perception of the intellectual and political convictions of Europe before 1914. Caught between a fascination with rational optimism and the mystical abandon to the dark and demonic, he resolves to live henceforth with a fuller understanding of the great existential tensions which are here, as so often in Mann's work, elaborated in a vast pattern of symbolic figures and events. *The Magic Mountain* is a spectacular tour de force; yet, when in 1929 Mann received the Nobel Prize, the award was not for this novel but for the more appealing *Buddenbrooks*.

Mann had worked twelve years on this expansive project. "Experiences were necessary for the writing of it which," he said at the time of its publication, "the author had in common with his nation and which had to be given artistic maturity, so as to appear at a favorable moment." The "favorable moment" was, of course, the historical and intellectual ferment which, in the Weimar Republic, followed Germany's defeat in the First World War. Mann's own share in the political life of the Twenties is demonstrated in several volumes of essays and addresses, but the writing of fiction remained his undiminished concern. In a "bourgeois novella," *Disorder and Early Sorrow* (1926), he treats in a most entertaining fashion the impact of revolution and inflation upon a family much like his own. *Mario and the Magician* (1930), again autobiographical in many of its details and a tale superbly told, is at once a political parable and a restatement of Mann's preoccupation with the artist as a "hero from weakness." By the fascination that emanates from his personality, the hunchback magician imposes his will upon the crowd and is shot by the hypnotized waiter Mario at the moment of his most intense exercise of power.

The story was to serve as a warning against the seduction and the exercise of ruthless power by fascism. It was written while Mann was at work on a new novel, *Joseph and his Brothers*, which differs in an important sense from all his earlier work. "It leaves behind the bourgeois individual sphere and enters into that of the past and the myth." The legend of Joseph and the patriarchal world in which it evolves, drawn from a variety of Old Testament sources, is explored, examined and retold in the terms provided by modern scholarship, archeology, psychology and theology. The mythical figure and its setting, both social and private, are here, by virtue of the narrator's painstaking testing and challenging of all available kinds of evidence, given the character of the typical and universal.

It is appropriate to the rendering of so elusive a topic as the fortunes of Joseph that the novelist should question again and again the premises of his own procedures: the book is interlarded with reflections not only on the facts brought together but on the narrator's own difficulties of obtaining these facts, of having to interpret unreliable texts, and, above all, of having to draw the reader into the experience of vast dimensions of time. The narrator's voice, employing a scale of humorous and serious, ironic and scholarly, moving and self-critical tones provides the coherent and constant tenor of the novel. *Joseph*, Thomas Mann wrote to his friend Erich Kahler, "is an epic jest, mankind's humorous fairy tale, and I believe that later generations will be surprised that such a work could be produced in our time."

The four volumes of *Joseph* were completed in 1943, during Mann's exile in the United States; two other projects were taking shape at the same time, both related to Mann's attachment to Goethe. One is the novel *The Beloved Returns*, completed in Princeton in October 1939, in which the now aging Charlotte, the celebrated heroine of Goethe's *The Sorrows of Young Werther*, pays a visit to the distinguished old man of letters. Once again Mann explores the puzzling and contradictory character of the artist, unattractive, self-centered and self-serving, but at the same time resolved to devote his life not to the "bliss of the ordinary" but to the detachment, the discipline, and the denial of self that are the price of genius. The novel is as witty as it is characteristic of Mann's evolving technique of using, often in subtly modified disguise, bits of Goethe's diaries, letters or conversations to form a mosaic of truth and fiction. Mann himself spoke of this book as "an impertinent anachronism" and was delighted when the British prosecutor at the Nuremberg trials quoted, as though it were an authentic saying of Goethe's, a passage which Mann had invented.

In January 1940, still in Princeton, Mann, following a suggestion by Heinrich Zimmer, the distinguished scholar of Indian mythology, began another novella, *The Transposed Heads*, "a Maya grotesque," he wrote to Agnes Meyer, "from the sphere of the cult of the Great Mother, in whose honor heads are cut off—a playful treatment of the problem of disjunction and identity —not very serious, at best a curiosity. . . ." The theme implied in this "iridescent and oscillating" piece is a reprise of a familiar notion: spirit and body, instinct and nature must remain separate and antithetical; they will not join, even in an act that has the blessing of divine beings.

The other major novel which he planned after completing work on *Joseph* was to occupy him for almost four years; it is the story of a modern Doctor Faustus, the fictional biography of a contemporary musician who achieves the ultimate in insight and artistry by surrendering to the devil: he is granted extraordinary powers of perception at the cost of the capacity to love. Leverkühn is the characteristic representative of art in our time. The complex structure of modern experience tends to paralyze creativity and to drive the artist into desperate regions beyond communication: Adrian Leverkühn's compositions are demonic and inaccessible to the point of being inhuman; they are beyond understanding and almost beyond expression. This life of ultimate solitude is related by a friend, the sensible humanist and "bourgeois" teacher of the classics, Serenus Zeitblom, a figure who provides the narrative distance from Leverkühn's barely comprehensible career. He writes his friend's biography at the time of the nearly total destruction of Germany, between 1943 and 1945—Mann's suggestion of the ominous parallel between Leverkühn's exorbitant spiritual reach and the perversion of a great culture into the exercise of limitless power. The novel is thus a conspectus of contemporary civilization, its social, philosophical, and aesthetic issues, far more radical, more profound, and more pessimistic than *The Magic Mountain*. It is demanding and moving at once—he was touched to learn that it brought tears into the eyes of many readers—and it is certainly the work which involved Mann himself most deeply. Erich Kahler, one of Mann's closest friends, speaks of *Doctor Faustus*, in a celebrated essay, as one of the great "terminal works" of our time, in which the Faust legend receives its valid, secularized modern form.

As he did in his earlier fiction, Mann here integrates miscellaneous materials drawn from biographies and correspondences of Nietzsche, Mahler, Wolf, Tschaikowsky and others into the web of the novel and makes use of the scholarly advice of distinguished friends such as Schönberg, Tillich, and Adorno. Through such "montage," he produces a work of astonishing resonance and of the sort of indirection and allusiveness which he has insisted is one of the inescapable features of modern fiction. In the sense that the novel, as any work of art today, must draw with critical detachment upon the total canon of previous thought and artistry, it is bound to become parodistic.

It is part of Mann's self-reflective view of the novelist's craft that in 1949 he recapitulates and reconstructs from diary entries, in a small book entitled *The Story of a Novel*, the circumstances that accompanied, between 1943 and 1946, the writing of this work. Until Mann's notebooks are published, this account presents one of the most detailed records of a novelist's creative preoccupations.

Mann's allusive manner, his fondness for "montage," for incorporating with subtle modifications materials from historical, theological or scientific works and of using, seriously or playfully, elements of an archaic or historically charged language, determines once more the mode of a short novel, *The Holy Sinner* (1951). Here, the medieval poem by Hartmann von Aue suggests the life history of Gregorius, the incestuous child who, after being brought up by a fisherman, is anxious to find his parents, wanders about and arrives in Bruges in time to defend, and marry, the queen, who is in fact his own mother. As a penitent sinner, he is in the end made a "very just" Pope before whom one day an old woman appears for confession: it is his mother and wife. What Mann tells in this charming prose narrative is the myth of the "elected" figure, of a sinner chosen and distinguished, who is made accessible to us, the sceptical modern readers, by Mann's "parodistic" use of the historical legend and of a language reminiscent of Hartmann. As in *Joseph* he sought here, through modern psychological and artistic procedures, to "amplify, realize and specify what is in fact a remote myth."

Two late novels conclude the rich canon of Mann's fiction—a strange tale, *The Black Swan* (1953), and the expanded version of the biography of a swindler, *The Confessions of Felix Krull, Confidence Man* (1954) with which, largely because of what seemed to him forbidding technical difficulties, he had been occupied for over forty years. The first of these is not easy to assess: it is the story of an aging woman, the mother of two children, who falls in love with an attractive and uncomplicated young American. Her passionate wish to give herself to Ken Keaton is cruelly and ironically frustrated by the discovery that her sudden renewal of vitality is not an indication of health, but of a fatal illness. If familiar antitheses of Mann's thinking seem here to recur, if the tension between disease and perception is once again stated in an elaborate parable, this is done with a compassion and a feeling for the triumph of happiness and the gift of grace that only a mind of serene maturity could achieve.

Felix Krull is a different matter: it is, in essential respects, the sum of Mann's work. What appears in the course of this most amusing "autobiography" to be merely a series of picaresque adventures of a rogue is, in fact, a highly stylized and carefully wrought portrait of the artist. Krull, carried by the unshakable belief that he is "cut from finer wood" than the indolent mass, and determined to enjoy life on his own terms, performs to the full all the splendid roles which he sets himself to act; he thinks, as he manages to evade the draft, that it is nobler to "act like a soldier" than merely to be one, to live up to his gifts as an irresistibly handsome lover than to involve himself in the serious banalities of ordinary relationships. He is Hermes when, as a waiter in an exclusive Paris hotel, he satisfies the hectic expectations of love of Mme Hupfle, and when he agrees to go on a journey around the world instead of—and as—the young Marquis de Venosta. His trip to Lisbon, his encounter with the paleontologist Kuckuck and his wife and daughter, and his presentation at Court are only the beginning of a career of radical idealism in a world in which all subjective efforts at transcending the unreflected life may well seem objectively criminal.

In the style of carefully calculated equanimity and as though parodying the traditional forms of the memoir and, particularly, the elevated classical prose of Goethe's *Poetry and Truth*, Mann creates Krull as the epitome of the amoral artist, fixed from the beginning in his character and dedicated to the conviction that appearance must transcend reality. The events of his life, in themselves absurd, and plausible only in the perspective of this undaunted idealist, are related in an elegant, precious and ambiguous language, in ironic professions of astonishment at the obtuseness of the world about him, and in understatements and amusingly perverted definitions of the judgments that justify and distinguish his inevitably eccentric existence. Krull, forty years old, writes these memoirs after his career has ended in prison. Mann's elaborate plans for the later parts of the novel were not realized.

To capture, to master the magic of life with ever greater refinement of sense and intelligence is Krull's single-minded purpose; again and again he asserts his calling and his destiny. What he means to gain is the most treasured prize of human effort: the attainment of spiritual freedom, the freedom not of commonplace action but of living symbolically. The resolution of the paradoxical tension between appearance and reality cannot be achieved in the course of his life, the life of Till Eulenspiegel, of Don Giovanni or even Faust. It is a resolution that may be accomplished only in the created myth of a work such as this final performance, which more than any of his previous novels, epitomizes the range and power of Thomas Mann's belief in the spirit.

It is no coincidence that at the end of his life, after publishing *Krull*, Mann should have devoted one of his most masterly addresses to the commemoration of Schiller. This speech, and the portrait of Krull, are pieces of ironic self-portraiture; the one solemn and dark, the other the very essence of Mann's entertaining gift for the projection of an ambiguous human situation. Both set forth the central theme of his fiction: the victory of perception over the compulsion of nature. Poet and swindler alike resist the confounding interplay of appearance and reality; both assert their resources of understanding and performance, however oblique, in order to achieve freedom. Krull, no less than Schiller, is the very image of the artist, the symbol of the creative human being.

Thomas Mann and the German Philosophical Tradition: Two Essays on Nietzsche

STANLEY CORNGOLD

Thomas Mann never tired of declaring his indebtedness to the German intellectual tradition, "the great unfolding of Germanism from Luther to Bismarck and Nietzsche." "What I owe to the German tradition of thought," he wrote, "and how deeply rooted I am in that tradition, is perfectly clear. . . ." Two aspects of his position are worth stressing. The first is the extreme importance which Mann assigns to tradition within the act of writing fiction. Criticized for the lack of "creative imagination" in his early work, Mann replied: "I say that very great writers did not invent anything in their whole lives, but merely poured their souls into traditional materials and reshaped them." Extreme as this formulation may sound, Mann never basically modified it. He saw his entire *oeuvre* as a reinterpretation of the cultural past. His work is less "the fragment of a great confession" than a monument (still living and ever changing) to the energy and interest of the German intellectual tradition.

The second remarkable aspect of his dependence on tradition is the fact that it has for him an intellectual and by no means an exclusively literary character. When, at the time of composing a kind of intellectual autobiography in his *Reflections of a Non-Political Man* (1918), he comes down to defining his essential tradition within the German past, that tradition turns out to be mainly a philosophical one. "The three names which I have to set down when I ask myself about the foundations of my intellectual and artistic development—these names for a triple constellation of eternally connected spirits—[are] Schopenhauer, Nietzsche, and Wagner." For Mann these figures in their succession constitute an objective historical development: "Their destinies as creators and dominators are profoundly and inseparably linked." But they are linked in another, more intimate way: "The three of them are one. The reverent disciple, for whom their mighty careers represent a culture, could wish to speak of them all simultaneously, so difficult does it seem to him to keep separate what he owes to each individually." Right from the outset, in this early passage, we see Mann effectively interiorizing, in coherent personal experience, the objective historical interconnectedness of these thinkers.

The remarks which follow aim to analyze part of the lifelong process by which Mann assimilated the work and personality of Nietzsche. This process is important in the sense that, as Mann wrote, "the experience of Nietzsche's criticism of culture and his stylistic artistry is of the first order of importance in my life." This process is important too because it illustrates in an exemplary way the close inner relation of Mann's political, artistic, and critical activity.

To explore with any thoroughness the Mann-Nietzsche nexus, one would have to attend to at least four non-fictional texts. They are the chapter "Introspection" in *Reflections of a Non-Political Man* (1918); Mann's speech on the occasion of a musical evening honoring Nietzsche in 1924 (the text is found in the German volume *Altes und Neues*, 1953); portions of *A Sketch of My Life* (1930, 1960), Mann's obligatory autobiography composed shortly after receiving the Nobel Prize for literature (1929); and finally the essay "Nietzsche's Philosophy in the Light of Recent History" (1947), Mann's revaluation of Nietzsche after the second world war. (This piece is found in *Last Essays*, 1959.) Furthermore, there are Mann's *Letters* (1971), which abound in references to Nietzsche and, of crucial importance, the novel *Doctor Faustus* (1947, 1948), which Mann called "something like a Nietzsche-novel," although the hero shares only certain traits with Nietzsche and others with Hugo Wolf and Mann himself.

The sense of Mann's changing attitude toward Nietzsche emerges most sharply from the contrast between his earliest and his latest essay, both written under the pressure of world wars. In the first, Mann is still the adulating disciple of the "educator" Nietzsche, whom he praises for his remarkable precision. In the second, Nietzsche is specifically declared "barren of all sense of pedagogic responsibility," and a good deal of his work is judged an insufferable "romanticizing of evil." But since "Nietzsche's Philosophy in the Light of Recent History," as well as all the later works, are readily available in English, it may be most useful to focus here on the two earlier works, which have not been translated.

In the *Reflections* Mann sees Nietzsche as par excellence a critic of the German character. The brilliance of his pronouncements on "the German question" suggests the passion of his concern. The word "passion" is key: for Mann it means, not blind love, but love frustrated by doubt, a mixture of love and criticism. As scathing as Nietzsche is toward the Germans, nowhere in this polemic, Mann asserts, can one find the contempt with which he speaks of other subjects—the English character, for example: English utilitarianism and English unmusicality. (If Nietzsche also criticizes France, he is less cruel, for the French are only the soldiers—and the sacrifices—of English ideas.) The point of Mann's argument is that Nietzsche's criticism of Germany is native and complex and has nothing in common with the clumsy moralizing of *Entente* democrats. The phenomenon of Nietzsche makes Germany interesting. Nietzsche educated the young Mann into a kind of "psychologically-oriented patriotism," an intellectual love of the nation that provokes passionate criticism.

What is crucial about anti-German criticism is its source and its tone. Nietzsche's own anti-Germanism arises within a highly developed "European" tradition to which Goethe, Schopenhauer, and Wagner belong. It was the "moral mood" of Schopenhauer and Wagner which attuned Mann to Nietzsche's moralism, his fundamentally German resistance to European decadence. Mann notes: "I well remember the smile, or was it the laugh, which I had to suppress, when one day Paris *literati*, whom I sounded out on Nietzsche, gave me to understand that *au fond* he had been nothing more than a good reader of the French moralists and aphorists. If at least they had mentioned Pascal. . . ." This sort of obtuseness profiled for Mann Nietzsche's essentially German character. "What could be more German than his contempt for the 'modern ideas,' 'the ideas of the eighteenth century' . . . , [more German] than 'that deep disgust' with which the German spirit itself rose up against the English-French world of ideas. . . . One sees how well Nietzsche understood Dostoevsky on the *recalcitrant* role of the German character in European intellectual history. . . . 'With deep disgust'. . . . There it is, the origin of this war, the German war against Western 'civilization'!"

Mann legitimizes the first world war on grounds provided by Nietzsche. Nietzsche is arch-German in the degree to which he opposed the "radicalism" of the Western democracies. Or to put the matter positively: Germany, because of its anti-radicalism and its "unliterariness," emerges as the "people of life." "The *concept of life*—it is this most German, most Goethean, and in the highest religious sense conservative idea that Nietzsche imbued with new feeling, clothed in a new beauty, force, and sacred innocence, elevated to the highest rank, and brought to spiritual dominance." Nietzsche's critique of decadence always speaks in the name of this ideal. This moment represents, for Mann, a unique origin, for until Nietzsche the bold temper of modern criticism had been inspired only by aestheticism. Nietzsche is the first to put moral ideals, indeed truth itself, into question by asking of the value of truth for life.

"Or did he perhaps only give beauty a new sacred, ecstatic name—that of life? And was, then, his rebellion against morality also more the rebellion of an artist and lover than of a genuinely philosophical spirit?" This surmise prompts Mann to speculate: Schopenhauer's philosophy proved a find for Wagner; his Tristan is full of the atmosphere of "Cross, Death, Tomb." Could not Nietzsche's philosophy similarly prove a lucky find to a great writer, "namely, as the source of a loftiest, crotically most cunning *irony*, playing between life and mind? . . . Nietzsche unlike Schopenhauer has not found or has not yet found his artist." The reader assumes that Mann means to suggest only ironically that he himself is this artist. But does not this ironical play precisely serve to qualify Mann as this sort of artist? In any case, however incompletely Mann knows his work to have accomplished this philosophy, his debt to Nietzsche is large and definite—"the idea of life . . . —an anti-radical, anti-nihilistic, anti-literary, a most conservative, a German idea . . . and yet . . . ."

There still remains the essential distinction to be drawn between Nietzsche's doctrine and the manner in which he taught it. For if his doctrine is German, his style is not. Nietzsche's language is that of the European intellectual, the type of the wordly prose writer, the feuilletonist of distinction whom, precisely, France and England excel at producing. His all-probing, all-dissolving style taught all of Europe, Germany included, how to write—how to criticize, how to be radical. Nietzsche's paradoxical importance for Germany has been not in his producing the new man of whom he spoke but the new man who would speak like him. "He influenced the intellectual life of Germany . . . at least, at the very least, as strongly as a prose-writer working in the European mold as through his 'militarism' and his philosophical idea of 'power'; and his 'progressive,' civilizing effect consists in an enormous strengthening, encouraging, and sharpening of the institution of the writer (*Schriftstellertum*), of the literary critical spirit, and of radicalism in Germany." Nietzsche's style cultivates an attitude of emulation of the dubious progressive spirit of the *Entente*. His educative example could not sustain the German mind.

Now, no one will find Mann's first essay on Nietzsche notably transparent. Mann detects Nietzsche's arch-Germanness in the fervor of his attack on the German character; this character Mann defines also as "an extremely remarkable, European element stimulating passionate criticism." Nietzsche's attack proceeds in the name of the ideal of life, whence his educative effect; but his main educative effect occurs through the medium of his style, which has heightened the presence, in another sense, of the "European element" in Germany. One might ask, what bearings, then, does Mann take from the psychological patriotism inspired in him by Nietzsche? The answer can only be ironical and oblique. Mann's own style of analysis in the passages above quite clearly emulates Nietzsche as a "Europeanizing" intellectual, in the very moment that Mann decries the dubious, un-German, and thus un-Nietzschean effects of such a mode. What Mann assimilates of Nietzsche at this point in his development is mainly a style and not a lucid criticism of culture.

The importance of Mann's second Nietzsche-essay (1924) is that it postdates his political and moral turn to the cause of the German republic. And if, as he would later write, "philosophy is not a cold abstraction but consists of experiencing, suffering, and sacrificing for humanity," then Mann, who suffered for his republican views, was now the more accurate philosopher. When now he calls Nietzsche an "educative spirit," he no longer intends the paradox of the *Meditations*. There education meant at once education toward and away from Europe; here education indubitably means the turn toward Europe, the German overcoming of the German past. It means this at the same time that Mann takes pains not to make it mean this too abruptly, too radically, too unpatriotically. The path of his argument is convoluted, but its basic sense is plain.

The decision to honor Nietzsche with music and not with speeches is crucial: to do so "is to acknowledge what he means to us today, namely, the way in which, precisely now, in this German and European hour, we feel him to be our moral master." It is in Nietzsche's relation to German music that Mann's audience must find a moral example. For Nietzsche, as we know, abandoned German music, though not light-heartedly, for he loved music as no one else: indeed "his language is itself music."

Mann's point is dialectical. He wants us to remember that when, for the sake of the future, Nietzsche abandoned German music, he gave up something of essential value. In the *Meditations*, too, Mann attributed a certain musicality to Nietzsche's language, but only as one among various qualities defining it as intellectual speech—the agile and acute instrument of the European critical voice. To continue to conceive of Nietzsche's language in this way would make his repudiation of the German musical character inevitable and possibly painless. But to see Nietzsche's style, instead, as fusing music and criticism, is finally to conceive him in a wholly different way. In *Meditations*, Mann had cited a magnificent line from a poem on Nietzsche by Stefan George: "Sie hätte singen, nicht reden sollen, diese neue Seele" ("It should have sung, not spoken, this new soul"). Mann had then gone on to comment that George had entirely missed the point: Nietzsche's voice was quintessentially one that did not sing. It spoke, in prose, and because it did, its effect had been dubious. Now, however, in Mann's second essay, "the phenomenon of Nietzsche reveals at the level of personal genius . . . the peculiar intimacy and inner unity of critique and *music*." And yet this intimacy does not preclude tension. Having asserted the affinity of the two terms, having brought them to the point of closest union, Mann must begin to separate them. The link of criticism and music is after all one of passion, and passion always includes the pain of doubt.

Doubt about what? Nietzsche's doubt about music, writes Mann, arose from the fact that he very nearly identified music with the romantic spirit and very nearly identified the romantic spirit with Germany. His fate was to oppose this powerful complex—and more. For Nietzsche to oppose meant to overcome himself; like Wagner, he too was a late-born son of German romanticism. "But Wagner was a mighty and fortunate self-glorifier and self-consummator, whereas Nietzsche was a revolutionary self-conqueror, with this result: Wagner remained only the last glorifier and infinitely fascinating consummator of an epoch, whereas Nietzsche became a seer and the leader into a new future for mankind."

In the *Meditations*, Nietzsche was seen attacking German philistinism in an intellectual style which ushers in a dubious future. Here, Nietzsche renounces the priority of music and so it must follow, of the musical element of his very language, to become, by virtue of his sacrifice, the prophet of a new German (Republican) future. "For the romantic is the song of homesickness for the past, the magic song of death; and the phenomenon of Richard Wagner, which Nietzsche loved so infinitely and which his ruling spirit had to overcome, was nothing more than the paradoxical and eternally interesting phenomenon of the world-conquering ecstasy of death." And he who "conquers death"? Such a figure merits the special irony of allegorical language, and this Mann promptly awards to Nietzsche, "the best son" of romanticism, who, "for us all, in his conquest, consumed his life and died—the new word on his lips which he barely knew how to utter, which we too barely know how to stammer, the prophetic word of friendship with life and future." He did betray Wagner, he became a Judas; but because he did so, "today everything that believes in the future swears by his name, and he has become the evangelist of a new covenant between man and the earth."

Mann's speech is so extraordinarily interesting because in it we watch him turning to his own purpose the German intellectual tradition as he conceived it. The tradition matters enormously to him since, at his own word, it is the substance of his art. He is less direct about asserting that it is also, in good measure, the substance of his life, that it supplies him with *types* by which to understand his actions and his work. In this speech Mann found a way of keeping himself intact as a disciple of Nietzsche and at the same time sustaining his new democratic position. He did this by reinterpreting his source.

No longer is Nietzsche the arch-German and unconscious dissolver of the German tradition. Instead he is a trans-historical, prophetic figure who heroically and consciously renounced the German tradition. But Mann, the self-acknowledged disciple of Nietzsche, is also the subject of this address. This point becomes perfectly clear in a letter Mann wrote to the composer Hans Pfitzner a year later. There he repeats almost word for word the language with which he distinguished the self-consummator Wagner from the self-conqueror Nietzsche. In what context? To create a perspective in which Pfitzner, the conservative Romantic composer, can grasp that posterity will not support his indictment of the alleged Judas, the republican Thomas Mann.

But we must beware of asserting too hastily that it is the exigency of Mann's life, the need for practical self-justification, that inspires his use of intellectual history. The line that links his life and his art is more complex. In a letter to Ernst Fischer (May 25, 1926), Mann perceives that the self-transcendence of Romanticism in Nietzsche is a constitutive feature of his *work*, indeed, the guarantor of its merit. "There is another element that links me with modernity and alone gives my work some validity on the intellectual plane: my experience with romanticism's self-transcendence in Nietzsche. What you feel to be fascinating . . . in my works is a critical distortion of fundamental instincts: irony."

Because of this evidence it is now clear that all terms in Mann's personal and artistic cosmos are equally privileged: his understanding of tradition, his novelistic practice, and his moral and political life. His ultimate refusal to assign a priority emerges finally in his allusion to Nietzsche in *A Sketch of My Life* (1930, 1960). Here Mann recalls the "great and decisive" experience of reading Nietzsche and Schopenhauer, but notes too that such experiences, if they are to be formative, presuppose a nature capable of being thus formed; and he will not undertake "to investigate the kind of organic assimilation and transformation to which, in [my] own case, Nietzsche's artistic and ethical character were subjected." Mann continues by remarking, quite accurately, that his experience of Nietzsche did not occur all at once, but was distributed in various phases over a number of years. The entire story of this rich and exemplary assimilation emerges only after mastery of Mann's entire *oeuvre*. The task awaits us, but the result of even this preparatory analysis should confirm Mann in his eloquent hope: "Even in these times it is possible for a man to construct out of his life and work a culture, a small cosmos, in which everything is interrelated, which, despite all diversity, forms a complete personal whole, and which stands more or less on an equal footing with the great life syntheses of earlier ages."

Thomas Mann as a Critic of Germany

THEODORE ZIOLKOWSKI

In the course of a public life lasting over half a century, Thomas Mann found himself accused, for various pronouncements on Germany, of political attitudes ranging from indifference and inconsistency through disloyalty to treason. During the first two decades of his career the young writer assumed a pose of fashionable aestheticism that was ostentatiously apolitical. When the events of World War I forced him to take a stand, he produced a rambling book entitled *Reflections of a Non-Political Man*, in which he attempted to justify German policies through a rather confused philosophy of cultural conservatism—a rationalization that infuriated liberals like his brother Heinrich and led to the estrangement of the two brothers. No sooner had the war ended, however, than his highly publicized lecture "The German Republic" caused conservatives to reproach him for repudiating his earlier loyalties. After the Nazis seized power in 1933, Mann was denounced by the émigrés and anti-Nazis for withdrawing his name from the list of contributors to the exile periodical *Die Sammlung* and for publishing the first two volumes of *Joseph and His Brothers* in Hitler's Germany. Yet by 1936 Mann had so antagonized the Nazis through various statements that his citizenship was revoked and the University of Bonn withdrew the honorary doctorate that had been awarded to Mann several years earlier. After World War II he was censured by the writers of the so-called "Inner Emigration" for his alleged desertion in Germany's hour of need and for his refusal to return as a spiritual leader of his country in its defeat. Yet when, in 1949, Mann not only returned to the Federal Republic but even went on to Weimar to collect the Goethe award of the German Democratic Republic, indignation reached new heights. Because of such experiences Mann was fond of quoting a remark by Erasmus: "It is my destiny to be stoned by both parties while I do my best to support both."

Even though Mann's political orientation, which moved almost 180 degrees around the ideological compass in the years from 1914 to 1945, suggests a certain inconsistency, his response to political circumstances was actually dictated by a guiding star that set a strikingly steady course: his vision of the cultural ideal. Mann was by nature and disposition anything but a political animal. Hermann Hesse, writing to his old friend on his seventy-fifth birthday, recalled the "political and moral innocence" that characterized both of them in 1904 when they first met. It was neither accident nor irony that inspired Mann to call his book of wartime essays *Reflections of a Non-Political Man*. And later his letters are filled with apologies to his friends whenever political writings keep him away from the literary work that he regarded as real and important.

To be sure, the events of history forced Mann increasingly to take a "political" stance and to lend his name to political causes. Yet it is a very strange kind of politics indeed that he practiced, which derived its principles and its examples neither from history nor current events but from such unlikely authorities as Dostoevsky, Nietzsche, Novalis, Walt Whitman, and Goethe! Mann's response to political occasions, in other words, is never narrowly "political" but rather more generally cultural: he judges every political situation by the degree to which it measures up to his cultural ideal. Characteristically, he regarded as his most telling indictment of Nazi Germany neither his "political" essays nor his wartime speeches, but a novel about Goethe (*The Beloved Returns*, 1939) in which he held up his cultural ideal as a mirror in which National Socialism could see its inadequacies reflected.

Mann's cultural ideal probably never existed outside of his own imagination: yet he is specific and consistent when he lists its characteristics. Basically, it amounts to a glorification of nineteenth-century bourgeois culture with its values inherited from romanticism, its sense of national pride, its underlying pessimism regarding human nature (in contrast to the eighteenth-century belief in progress), and its compensating sense of humor or irony. It is a condition that Mann defines as Culture in contrast to Civilization on the French model: it glorifies Art as opposed to mere "literature," it prizes the integrity of the individual above the exigencies of society, it is militantly apolitical, and its exemplary hero is Richard Wagner.

Mann saw Germany as the source and site of this cultural ideal because he regarded Germany as the "land of the middle" between the extremes of Western rationalism and Eastern mysticism. In his *Reflections of a Non-Political Man* he argued that it is Germany's national destiny to be the battleground of Europe—not just geographically but spiritually as well. The spiritual conflicts of Europe, he says, will be settled in Germany's soul. In *The Magic Mountain* (1924) Settembrini tells Hans Castorp much the same thing: "*Caro amico!* There will be decisions to make, decisions of unspeakable importance for the happiness and the future of Europe; it will fall to your country to decide, in her soul the decision will be consummated. Placed as she is between East and West, she will have to choose, she will have to decide finally and consciously between the two spheres."

Now, in order to appreciate the significance of Mann's cultural vision, it is necessary to understand that it did not result from a cool and rational analysis of history and culture: instead, it amounts to a projection onto a national scale of intense personal needs. Mann regarded himself, as he wrote to Stefan Zweig in 1925, as a "genius of the golden mean." In 1934 he told Karl Kerényi that "I am a man of equilibrium: I lean instinctively to the left if the boat threatens to capsize to the right—and vice versa." This quest for balance, which manifests itself in an almost instinctive opposition to all extremes—in life and art, as well as politics—is basically a psychological need given in substantial measure by Mann's biographical circumstances.

The son of a North German merchant and senator and an exotic mother from South America, Mann sought throughout his life to reconcile in his own personality what he regarded as the competing claims of North and South: order and profligacy, intellect and passion, the spirit and the senses. The name of his early hero, Tonio Kröger, with its juxtaposition of the Teutonic and the Mediterranean, symbolizes onomastically this congenital tension. Similarly, in *The Magic Mountain* Hans Castorp finds that his mind has become the arena in which his two mentors, the rationalist Settembrini and the mystic Naphta, act out their struggle for control of his soul. At this point we begin to sense the amazing psychological consistency of Mann's cultural vision, which is rooted in the compelling need for equilibrium in his own life. It can be expressed most concisely in a syllogism, whose major premise is for Mann an item of faith: Mann is prototypically German; Mann's psyche is the battleground of reason and volition, of North and South (or East and West); therefore Germany is also a "land of the middle."

Seen in this light, Mann's allegedly "political" positions turn out to be anything but political in the strict sense of the word:

instead, they are reactions to current events determined emotionally (and almost irrationally) by his urgent need for balance and equilibrium. Whenever the political reality seemed to be moving too far away from his cultural ideal, he threw his weight and moral authority to the other side. During World War I, in reaction against German intellectuals who seemed to be rushing to such an extreme of Western liberalism that they threatened to desert the German values that Mann treasured, he wrote an ultraconservative book in an attempt to right the cultural and political ship of state. When the Nazis seized power and tried to mislead the people through a misapplication of Germanic myth and romantic ideas, Mann took the opposite point of view and appealed to reason and democracy. It is this quest for balance that establishes the rhythm underlying the superficially wild swings of Mann's political pendulum.

When the events of World War I first jolted Mann out of his rather haughty aestheticism into a political decision, he instinctively took the side of his homeland. But this "political" choice was subsequently motivated by his conclusion that the traditional German monarchy was more conducive than Western democracy to the preservation of Culture as he had defined it. For Culture in Mann's sense depends upon absolute freedom; and—this is Mann's paradoxical reasoning—when Art is reduced to the service of a political cause, as is the case in democratic states, the moment that it becomes *engagé*, it is no longer free "poetry" but mere applied literature. Politics, Mann argued, is alien and destructive to the German character, which thrives upon inner freedom of the sort provided by monarchy rather than within the demanding social organization afforded by democracy. To the extent that democracy requires the political participation of the individual, it inhibits true inner freedom. For this reason Mann insisted that the democracy preached by the Allies represented a grave threat to all the ideals of German culture as he knew and valued it. As a result, he sides with Germany in World War I both "with his heart" and by intellectual choice.

The spokesman of German conservatism rapidly lost his following, however, when he concluded shortly after the war that the old forms of government no longer constituted the best framework for his ideal of culture. The audience that first heard Mann's talk on "The German Republic" in 1922 shuffled its feet and muttered its discontent as Mann outlined his new view of a cultural republic—again based on a curious amalgam of Romantic and Modern, the German and the Western, Novalis and Walt Whitman. It is important to recognize that Mann has not altered his cultural ideal: but now that he envisages its realization in a different manner, his political stance shifts. From this point on he begins to speak about a "new humanism" comprising a synthesis of political and cultural life, of individualism and social responsibility, that will be achieved in the new Republic of Germany, which he still regards as the "land of the middle."

By 1933 it had become clear to Mann that his cultural ideal was not going to be realized in Germany, which had now fallen into the hands of the National Socialists. His lecture on "The Suffering and Greatness of Richard Wagner," which aroused great dissatisfaction among the Nazis, was in fact an elegy to the vanishing ideals of the nineteenth-century bourgeois culture that was being exploited and debased in the service of politics. In such writings as "The Coming Victory of Democracy," which Mann delivered many times as a lecture in the United States, he made it clear that he saw in Western democracy the best chance of realizing the cultural ideal that, only twenty years earlier, he had seen most adequately represented by the monarchy of Kaiser Wilhelm.

Inevitably, as Mann came to anticipate the actualization of his cultural ideal in Western democracy, he began to express an increasing disenchantment with Germany for having disappointed his expectations so grievously. As a result, the cultural ideal that began as an idealized reflection of nineteenth-century German society was liberated to become more generally European. Mann's letters during the forties are characterized by an ambivalence toward the Germans—a bitterness exacerbated by the love that he still felt for the memory of his homeland. Toward the end of the war (October 20, 1944), he wrote to Erich Kahler that his *dégoût* for everything German was growing enormously. "An impossible, a hopeless race, truly *une race maudite*. They have learned nothing, understand nothing, regret nothing." A year later (December 15, 1945) he wrote to his brother Viktor that the Allies were making mistakes in their treatment of the Germans, who regard humane treatment as weakness and brood over severity as though it were revenge. A few months later (April 1, 1946) he continued in the same vein to Viktor, saying that the Germans' inherent tendency to feel insulted was now degenerating into a wholly pathological irritability. And on January 12, 1947, he wrote to Félix Bertaux that it was his impression that the Germans had neither learned nor forgotten a thing. "Nationalism, antisemitism, a stupid neofascism are burgeoning, and in the intellectual sphere, among students and intellectuals, there prevails a kind of nihilism that in calmer times might be regarded as 'interesting,' but that under present-day conditions represents an irresponsible threat to civilization and humanity."

At the same time, Mann steadfastly refused—both during and after the war—to succumb to the facile suggestion that there are really two Germanies—a good Germany in exile and an evil one back at home. The bad Germany, he insisted in numerous articles and letters, was simply the good Germany gone astray. Thus he warned Kahler (May 1, 1945) that "We must not go around describing ourselves as the 'good' Germany, in contrast to the 'wicked' Germany with which we supposedly had nothing to do. The 'wicked' is the 'good' Germany whose goodness turned to wickedness." Clearly, this dialectical explanation is wholly consistent with Mann's view of Germany as the "land of the middle" where all forces are locked in struggle.

It was Mann's urgent sense of identity with Germany and all of its qualities, good and bad alike, that enabled him to experience its horror along with the glory of its culture. "This Man Is My Brother" is the title of an essay in which he attempted to explain Hitler to the American people: Hitler's charisma, he suggested, lay in the fact that he appealed to many of the same values as Mann himself, though in a debased and trivialized form (e.g., Wagner's music, Nietzsche's philosophy, and Romantic myth). He concluded his lecture on "Germany and the Germans" (1945) by stressing to his audience that he knows all these things about Germany's huge potential for evil because "I also have it within me, I have experienced it all in my own body." No one sees more clearly than a lover betrayed; and when Germany jilted Mann and his ideals for the cheap allure of Hitler, Mann scrutinized his beloved country's shortcomings with a merciless eye.

In an open letter explaining "Why I Cannot Return to Germany" Mann pointed out that it was an inherent and ancient German temptation to sign pacts with the devil—a tendency foreshadowed in Germany's principal contribution to world myth, the legend of Faust. Appropriately, Mann made his most incisive statement about Germany not in his "political" writings but in the novel *Doctor Faustus* (1947), in which the fate of the composer Adrian Leverkühn, who signs a pact with Satan in order to write great music, is paralleled by the rise and fall of the Third Reich. The tension of love and horror with which Mann regards his hero reflects precisely the ambivalence of his attitude toward Germany—the "bad" Germany that is nothing more than the "good" Germany in a state of guilt and decline.

Yet the sense of close identification, the act of projection that enabled Mann to detect all aspects of his own problematical psyche in the history of Germany, also made it possible for him to retain his faith in German culture even when Germany as a political entity was arousing the abhorrence of the civilized world. For Mann refused to identify culture and politics. As he wrote to the Rector of Bonn University in 1937, the leaders of Germany "have the incredible audacity to confuse themselves with Germany" while in reality they had succeeded in ruining Germany both spiritually and physically. From the very start of his career Mann had been keenly conscious of his public image, of what he called the "representative" responsibilities of his life as a writer. It was this conviction of his own representative significance as an embodiment of German culture that sustained Mann during the years of his political exile. In 1936 he notified the German Information Agency that the Nazis could not harm him by withdrawing his citizenship. "I have already explained at an earlier time that I have deeper roots in German life and tradition than the temporary, though subtly penetrating, figures who at present are ruling in Germany." As he was fond of saying during his years in the United States, "Where I am is Germany."

Paradoxically, as Mann became increasingly critical of Germany and secure in his own mission as a representative of German culture, his cultural ideal—originally "Made in Germany" —was located more and more in a province of the imagination that was detached from any real geographical land. Ultimately, of course, no country on earth could possibly live up to his expectations. Unable to bring himself to return to Germany after the war, yet disaffected by political and cultural conditions in the United States, Mann spent the last years of his life in Switzerland, where he could gaze across the nearby borders in futile search of the vanished Germany of his youth, now quite literally a Mann without a Country.

Thomas Mann and the Emigré Intellectuals

THEODORE ZIOLKOWSKI

Shortly after Hitler became Chancellor of the Reich, Thomas Mann left Germany on a lecture tour. So he was safely out of the country on February 27, 1933, when the Reichstag fire provided the National Socialists with an excuse to seize absolute powers. Warned that he was on the Nazi list of those guilty of "intellectual high treason," Mann decided not to return to Germany. After a few months on the Riviera, the Manns settled down at Küsnacht near Zurich. For the next three years Mann maintained an ambivalent attitude toward Germany and his fellow émigrés. Although he declined membership in the *Reichsschrifttumskammer* (Literary Chamber of the Reich), he avoided any public anti-Nazi statements and continued to publish his works in Germany. Despite his friendship with many of the German refugees who passed through Zurich, he was skeptical of all efforts, such as those of his brother Heinrich, to organize the émigrés into an effective political unit; and he refused to become associated with the exile periodical *Die Sammlung*, which was edited by his son Klaus Mann, lest his right to publish in Germany be withdrawn.

It was not until 1936 that Mann finally and firmly declared himself to be on the side of the émigrés. In January of that year the Swiss journalist Eduard Korrodi published an article in the *Neue Zürcher Zeitung* in which he argued that the German émigré literature was almost exclusively a Jewish affair. In his response of February 3, Mann pointed out that neither he and his brother Heinrich, nor many of the other prominent exile writers—e.g., Bertolt Brecht and Johannes R. Becher—were Jewish and yet these writers were just as profoundly affected by the emigration and had often sacrificed just as much as the Jewish exiles. Through this widely publicized letter, which provoked the Nazis to withdraw his citizenship later that year, Mann announced his solidarity with the swelling ranks of intellectual émigrés from fascist tyranny and, at the same time, emerged as their leading spokesman.

Mann had always been keenly aware of his "representative"

responsibilities. But for the first sixty years of his life he had restricted his representation largely to the embodiment of German culture. Now he increasingly assumed the responsibility of speaking politically for his fellow émigrés. Once he had made up his mind to become their representative, Mann was indefatigable in his activities, both in Europe and the United States. In 1937 he became co-founder and co-editor of the journal *Mass und Wert* (*Measure and Value*), an undertaking to which he was actively committed until 1940. In his Foreword to the first volume Mann wrote: "We want to be artists and anti-barbarians, to venerate moderation, to defend values. . . ." It was in part the function of the new journal to jolt the German émigrés out of their "delusion that it is possible to be a non-political person of culture"—a delusion that Mann himself had shared for so many decades. In April 1937, Mann gave a speech at the New School for Social Research to celebrate the fourth anniversary of the Graduate Faculty of Political and Social Science, whose purpose it was "to preserve the institution of the German University, in spite of the inevitable dispersal of the German intellectuals all over the world, and to refound it here, beyond the seas." A few days later he spoke on the occasion of the establishment of the American Guild for German Cultural Freedom. He pointed out that the Guild was based on the assumption that the circumstances that had driven so many German intellectuals from their land were not unalterable, but only an unfortunate episode. It is the responsibility of the émigrés, he concludes, "to carry the living German spirit through night and winter, to keep its flame alive for better days." In 1938 Mann made still another trip to the United States, traveling this time to many cities with his lecture on "The Coming Victory of Democracy."

Largely as a result of the German annexation of Austria, which took place in March 1938 while he was on his fourth trip to the United States, Mann decided to give up his residence in Switzerland and move to this country. This was a significant move, which in many respects marked a new era in his relationship to the German émigré intellectuals. In his recent book *The Sea Change* (1975) H. Stuart Hughes notes that "the migration to the United States of European intellectuals fleeing fascist tyranny has finally become visible as the most important cultural event— or series of events—of the second quarter of the twentieth century." Now roughly two-thirds of these émigrés were of German or Austrian origin, and most of these were delighted to have as their more or less official spokesman a figure as widely recognized as the Nobel Prize winner Thomas Mann, who enjoyed a particular popularity in the United States.

No sooner did Mann get established in Princeton than he set to work: signing affidavits, working with such relief groups as the Emergency Rescue Committee, obtaining money and jobs for the émigrés. (See the letter to David Riesman of March 27, 1940.) As he wrote to his publisher, Gottfried Bermann Fischer, "My correspondence . . . has swollen alarmingly, until no less than three people must help me with it." Mann was a voluminous correspondent; it is estimated that he wrote no fewer than twenty thousand letters during his lifetime. Many of these letters were written during the years in exile—not just the practical correspondence to help needy colleagues, but also the symbolic letters through which Mann kept in touch with fellow émigrés all over the world: Hermann Hesse, Karl Kerényi, Johannes R. Becher, and many others. The index of Mann's published correspondence resembles a rollcall of prominent German émigrés.

During his two years in Princeton and, later, after his move to California, Mann also remained in personal contact with a large number of émigrés. In Princeton he was in close touch with such local residents as Albert Einstein, Erich Kahler, and Hermann Broch, as well as many new arrivals for whom the house on Stockton Street provided an initial point of orientation in the United States. In Pacific Palisades the record of his days includes frequent sessions with the growing colony of émigrés: Max Reinhardt, Theodor W. Adorno, Bruno Walter, Arnold Schönberg, Franz Werfel, Lion Feuchtwanger, Bruno Frank, Bertolt Brecht, and a host of others whose names now decorate the histories of modern German literature, music, art, and philosophy.

In addition to these personal contacts, Mann extended his range of influence through members of his own family: his son Golo, the historian and co-editor of *Mass und Wert*; his son Klaus, editor of the journal *Decision* and author of one of the finest novels of the emigration, *Der Vulkan* (*The Volcano*, 1939); and his daughter Erika, cabaret actress and journalist. All three traveled around the globe, first privately and then as war correspondents, creating a network of information and communication that revolved around Thomas Mann. And through his daughter Elisabeth, who had married the prominent Italian intellectual Giuseppe Antonio Borgese, Mann had contacts with the antifascist émigrés from Italy as well.

Thomas and Katia Mann with Klaus, Erika, and baby Golo at their country house in Bad Tölz, south of Munich, 1909

Katia Mann in Munich, 1915

Thomas Mann with his daughter Elisabeth, the child "heroine" of *Disorder and Early Sorrow*

Thomas Mann in Prague, 1922

The Mann house at Poschingerstrasse 1, Munich

Klaus with the dog Lux, Elisabeth, Michael, Katia, Thomas, and Golo Mann

Thomas Mann on a lecture tour in the United States, circa 1940

Letter to Erich Kahler: "I have taken up the ancient *Felix Krull* once again. . . . I suspended work on it in 1911 to write *Death in Venice* . . . [and] have actually resumed on the very same page in the Munich manuscript."

Thomas Mann in Kilchberg, 1955

Thomas and Katia Mann in Pacific Palisades California, circa 1950

Katia Mann at her husband's grave in the cemetery at Kilchberg, Switzerland

Of course, Mann himself was not sedentary during these years. The letterheads of his correspondence display a dizzying array of place-names—from the Savoy Hotel in London to the Hotel Durant in Berkeley, from the R.M.S. *Westerdam* of the Holland-America Line to the Library of Congress, where Mann held a sinecure as Consultant in Germanic Literature. The postmarks suggest the frantic pace that Mann kept up—first shuttling between Europe and the United States and then, subsequently, back and forth between East Coast and West Coast, explaining German culture to American audiences, preaching solidarity to German groups, representing Germany in exile to the many prominent Americans with whom he was in frequent touch. Finally, Mann was the obvious figure to speak for the émigrés to the Germans who had remained in Hitler's land. From 1940 to 1945 Mann recorded for the BBC a series of fifty-five radio broadcasts in which he explained the emigrants' view of the war and political affairs to the German people.

Inevitably, this representative activity manifested itself in Mann's creative work, which he maintained at a constant pace even in the midst of the turmoil of the war years. The first major work of the exile period, *The Beloved Returns* (1939), reflects the emigration only indirectly to the extent that this novel about Goethe embodies the cultural ideals that the émigrés were blindly bent on upholding. The connection is far more explicit, however, in the last volume of the tetralogy *Joseph and His Brothers*. It is well known that the various reforms instituted by Joseph in *Joseph the Provider* are based upon F. D. R.'s New Deal, which Mann had observed with great admiration after his arrival in the United States. But there is more to it. In a lecture on "The Joseph Novels" that he delivered at the Library of Congress in 1942, Mann spoke of the symbolic value of the fact that his tetralogy—begun in Germany, continued in Switzerland, and transplanted to America—is actually also an epic of emigration. The European migration to America had traditionally sprung from what Goethe called the "alleviation for humanity" effected by the American war of liberation. "But the measure and the significance which this flight and migration has assumed at present are something new. The diaspora of European culture which we are witnessing, the arrival of so many of its bearers, representatives of all categories of science and art, to these shores" will contribute, Mann believed, to "a new feeling of humanism" and to "the unification of the earth." Even as an author, then, Mann remained the spokesman of the emigration: by an act of fictional transformation Mann and his fellow émigrés have become Joseph and his brothers, come to bring their knowledge and culture to the New Egypt.

Indeed, the mood of the émigrés during their first years in the United States was rather messianic. Regarding themselves as the bearers of conscience and culture, Mann and his compatriots were sometimes peeved because they were not consulted by their new hosts. Thus Mann wrote to Erich Kahler shortly after Pearl Harbor (December 31, 1941) that "Americans are having bitter experiences. They never really believed in ours; at bottom they thought we were telling atrocity stories. How could we help laughing bitterly when Hull said of the last Japanese note that such lying and deceit had never happened before? It happened twenty-five times before, but no one wanted to or could recognize it." In general, Mann's letters to his fellow-émigrés reveal a degree of rancor that he managed to subdue in his public utterances. For instance, in a talk before the American Rescue Committee, Mann sketched the role of the refugees in the United States. He concedes that many of the émigrés had been received with honor and, in certain cases, with considerable financial emoluments. (At Princeton, Mann himself was paid a full professor's salary for delivering three public lectures and two course lectures per year. And at the Library of Congress he received a salary—$4900—that amounted to more than the average American income at the time.) But he complains that their presence had no practical political consequences. "On the contrary, we could not rid ourselves of the feeling that we represented for our hosts a certain burden, and specifically a psychic burden inasmuch as we represented an appeal to their conscience." In a letter to Erich Kahler (May 25, 1941) he speaks more frankly. "My speech is ready and recounts quite bluntly what stupidity, baseness, and ignorance we exiles have had to endure from the world for eight long years. I must say, I am looking forward to getting this off my chest."

Because of their almost totally germanocentric orientation the émigrés were blind, to a notable extent, to the realities of the American political and diplomatic situation. For instance, in a letter of February 9, 1942, Mann solicits the signature of Albert Einstein for a petition addressed to President Roosevelt; Mann is disturbed about the status of "enemy alien" that has been imposed temporarily upon many of the German émigrés. What this affair displays is the narrowly European attitude of a German writing from California who did not include in his appeal any reference to the plight of the many Japanese who were subjected at the same time to far sterner measures. And the correspondence betrays a lack of understanding for the situation on the East Coast, where a highly organized and active Fifth Column of resident Germans was beginning to move into action.

Mann, of course, was not blind to the unrealistic expectations of some émigrés. As he wrote to Kahler (May 25, 1941), "You have given an example of fortitude that honorably differs from the complete incompetence of most refugee intellectuals faced with their new situation. None of them, I have the impression, is prepared to learn anything new; rather they all want to go on as they did in times now buried, and expect roasted squabs to fly into their mouths." Yet Mann's annoyance at his failure to have a greater impact on public policy in the United States—despite his complaints before, during, and after the war of the "childish and well-meaning zeal" of the Americans that kept interfering with his private work—is representative of the mood of many German émigré intellectuals.

In short, Mann was the representative German, the symbolic figurehead of the German refugees, in every respect—both good and bad. He embodied the finest cultural ideals of Germany, and at the same time he was subject to the sometimes arrogant insularity of a privileged group that failed to appreciate the complexities of the new situation into which they found themselves transposed. As long as the war lasted, Mann and the other émigrés were locked into an uneasy truce with a host country that they did not fully understand and whose culture they regarded as inferior to the European nineteenth-century bourgeois culture that they retained so nostalgically in their memories. But once the war was over—the war in Europe, that is, for the émigrés cared little for the events in the Pacific—the situation began quite rapidly to change. On December 29, 1945, Mann wrote rather despondently to Kahler that "Fascism is not downed, is not beaten; there is no intention of defeating it. Instead it is engaged in steady growth, in Europe, here, everywhere. The change of mood to pro-German and hence anti-exile is highly interesting." In retrospect, he concedes reluctantly, "What a good period the war was!" Nothing could reveal more clearly than this shocking statement how utterly self-centered many of the émigrés were in political judgments.

The Cold War marked the end of the long truce between the United States and the émigrés, many of whom began hurrying back to Europe as soon as it was possible. A number of the émigrés, who out of simple political naiveté had become associated with various Communist front organizations, were indignant when during the McCarthy era they were questioned by the House Un-American Activities Committee and similar investigating agencies. In a letter to Kahler (January 2, 1952) Mann refers to "this country, with its moronic and persecution-mad atmosphere." As a result, and taking shrewd advantage of the Swiss-American tax agreement "which protects American citizens living in Switzerland from double taxation," Mann began his final representative act as a German émigré: the return to a Europe that had been altered so profoundly since 1933—not just by the war, but by the development of society altogether—that the newly returned Europeans scarcely recognized it. In a letter of April 14, 1951, Kahler had tried to persuade Mann that it was pointless to return to Europe. "In this connection I must tell you a little anecdote that illustrates our situation. Two friends are crossing the Atlantic, one sailing from Europe to America, the other from America to Europe. In the middle of the ocean the ships meet and pass. The friends standing at the rail recognize one another, and both call across the water simultaneously, 'Are you crazy?'" Mann appreciated the joke, which he passed on to several of his friends. Yet in his opinion, as he replied to Kahler a few days later, "the man sailing westward is just a trace crazier." In general, he concluded, "the European mentality does not come up to the barbarous infantilism we have here." And on this note Mann, the representative German émigré, left the country that had sheltered him for fourteen years to return to a Europe that existed only in his memory.

Thomas Mann in Exile

VICTOR LANGE

Among the many German and Austrian writers who left their native lands during the early years of the Nazi regime to settle in the United States, Thomas Mann was the most conspicuous. A figure of distinction, though by no means without literary and political detractors, he had played an important role in the cultural life of the Weimar Republic. In February 1933 he had delivered an address at the University of Munich commemorating the fiftieth anniversary of Wagner's death, and left soon afterwards to repeat the lecture in Amsterdam, Brussels, and Paris. The tenor of this address was political only by implication: instead of pronouncing a single-minded eulogy of a national hero, it offered a subtle analysis of a psychologically complex representative of nineteenth-century pessimism. A group of eminent Munich citizens (among them Richard Strauss, Hans Pfitzner and Hans Knappertsbusch) condemned Mann's critical view of Wagner and, by passing a resolution, initiated an increasingly vicious campaign which persuaded Mann, for the time being, to remain abroad. It was a decision not lightly taken: "I am much too good a German, much too closely attached to the cultural traditions and the language of my country, not to realize that the thought of exile over a period of years or even a life-time would have a serious, indeed a fatal, meaning for me."

He was not to see Germany again for sixteen years. Parts of his library and certain manuscripts were shipped to him in Switzerland; he resumed work on the *Joseph* novel, of which the first two volumes appeared in 1933 and 1934, and was anxious not to jeopardize the free circulation of his works in Germany. At the end of May 1934, he paid his first, brief visit to the United States, welcomed warmly by his American publisher, Alfred Knopf, and spectacularly by the press: he lunched with the editors of *The New York Times* and *The Nation,* and was feted at a testimonial dinner for 300 guests by Mayor LaGuardia and Columbia University President Nicholas Murray Butler, as well as a host of literary figures, among them Willa Cather, Sinclair Lewis, and H. L. Mencken.

The political climate in Germany continued to deteriorate, and the death of his German publisher, S. Fischer, increased Mann's fears that his work might soon be banned in Germany. A collection of essays, *Suffering and Greatness of the Masters*, was published in March 1935, his last volume until 1946 to appear under a German imprint. Shortly after his sixtieth birthday in June 1935, he visited the United States again to accept, together with Albert Einstein, an honorary degree at Harvard and to dine at the White House. The warmth and a certain solemnity of his reception were decisive factors in favor of his eventual residence in the United States.

His *Stories of Three Decades* (1936) was an enormous success in America and England; the third volume of the tales of *Joseph* was published, not in Germany but in Austria. Mann became a Czech citizen in November of that year and a few weeks later was officially informed of the loss of his German citizenship, as well as of the honorary degree which the University of Bonn had awarded him in 1919.

On his third trip to the United States he was the guest of the New School for Social Research; in an address in New York he declared his solidarity with the victims of fascism, and, most important for his future effectiveness in the United States, he met Eugene and Agnes Meyer, the publishers of *The Washington Post*, who urged him to settle in the United States and subsequently supported his application for an immigration visa. His later correspondence with Agnes Meyer is remarkably lively and telling.

Early in 1938 he began the first of several extensive lecture tours: in fifteen American cities he delivered his most unequivocal declaration in favor of a democratic world order, "The Coming Victory of Democracy." The thought of having to leave Europe permanently was much on his mind; yet "What is it, to be without a native land? My native land is in the work that I carry with me. Absorbed in it I feel all the warmth of being at home. My works are of the language, German speech and thought, the substance of a native tradition to whose development I have contributed. Where I am is Germany." On May 5 he entered the United States from Canada as a permanent resident. One of his most devoted admirers in the United States, Caroline Newton, offered her house at Jamestown, R.I., as a temporary residence. A few weeks later he received an invitation from President Dodds to serve at Princeton University as "Lecturer in the Humanities" during the coming academic year, to give two "conferences" in the Department of Modern Languages—on Goethe's *Faust* and on *The Magic Mountain*—and to deliver three public lectures. Mann accepted, and after a brief return to Europe, settled down at 65 Stockton Street in Princeton.

He was delighted with the town: "The place is something like a park, well suited for walks, with superb trees which now, at Indian summer time, glow in the most splendid colors. At night you can hear the leaves drop like rain, but they say that this serene autumn weather may prevail until Christmas and that the winter will be short" (to Erich Kahler, October 19, 1938). His lectures in Alexander Hall drew large audiences; with extraordinary regularity and determination he wrote the major part of a new novel *The Beloved Returns*, from which he read on several occasions to a distinguished circle of Princeton friends. "I am resolved to carry on my life and work as ever before, with the greatest perseverance, unaltered by events that may damage, but cannot disconcert or humiliate me" (to E.K., October 19, 1938). On May 18, 1939, he was awarded an honorary degree by Princeton University, and on the following day he joined Einstein to speak at the Princeton Theological Seminary. His appointment was renewed for the spring semester, 1940. *The Beloved Returns* was finished at the end of October 1939 and appeared two months later in Stockholm: his German readers did not see this or subsequent works until after the end of the war. A new novel, *The Transposed Heads*, preoccupied him during the first half of 1940.

As he was clearly the most prominent spokesman for the growing group of German refugee intellectuals and artists, throughout 1940 political and literary concerns, public appearances, and an ever more extensive correspondence made increasingly severe demands on his time. He was involved in the work of the Emergency Rescue Committee which enabled a number of German writers, among them Alfred Döblin and Franz Werfel, to leave Europe. Every month he delivered a BBC broadcast to German listeners; his lectures on "War and Democracy" and "The Rebirth of Democracy" projected his hopes for a humane social order in the post-war world.

The winter was filled with an astonishing series of social and political engagements, crowned, on January 14 and 15, 1941, by a visit to the White House, "where we were received with amazing distinction. The dizzying climax was cocktails in President

Roosevelt's study. He once again impressed me greatly; or rather, he rekindled my sympathetic interest in him: this mixture of cunning, sunniness, being spoiled, delight in being liked, and honest faith is hard to characterize. But he is somehow blessed and I am devoted to this—as it seems to me—born counter-figure to what is doomed."

Princeton seemed at times too close to New York and Washington, and during a brief visit to California, Mann bought a lot in Pacific Palisades on which to build a house. He gave up his Princeton appointment, and in March 1941 moved to California, his home for the next twelve years.

Berkeley awarded him an honorary degree, an occasion he described with undisguised pride in letters to his Princeton friend Erich Kahler and to Caroline Newton. In Pacific Palisades he was to live much as in Princeton, dividing his carefully organized time between his writing and the demands made upon him by countless organizations, acquaintances, and friends who were anxious to enlist the help of the most visible and most eminent among the European refugees. He was aware that his stature as a European man of letters, the success of his books in Mrs. Lowe-Porter's skillful, if often summary, translations, even his appointment, through Mrs. Meyer, as Consultant at the Library of Congress, distinguished him from countless German artists whose mode of life was far more precarious. On February 9, 1942, he urged Einstein to join a group of noted Europeans in asking President Roosevelt to make a distinction among "enemy aliens," between "potential enemies of American democracy . . . and the victims and sworn foes of totalitarian evil. . . ."

His chief concern remained his writing: the final volume of the *Joseph* story was the topic of a lecture given at the Library of Congress in November 1942, introduced by Vice President Wallace. That rich and slow-moving fictional biography was completed in January 1943 and published in Stockholm at the end of that year. As soon as *Joseph* was out of the way, Mann turned in March 1943 to a subject matter that was to occupy the next four years of his life. It was the story of a modern, Faustian musician, who by his pact with the devil, at the cost of total isolation, achieves the supreme capacity of articulating the modern analytical sensibility. Friends and neighbors, Bruno Walter, Feuchtwanger, Werfel, Schoenberg, Rubinstein, Křenek, Stravinsky, Hanns Eisler, Klemperer and, especially, Theodor Wiesengrund-Adorno contributed to the steady growth of this, Mann's "most daring and ominous" novel.

The political events of those months find their reflection in a lecture entitled "War and the Future" which he delivered in a number of cities in the East. "In Montreal," he wrote to Agnes Meyer, "the police had to be called, as the crowds could not get in and threatened to push in the doors. I ask myself: What do these people expect? I am no Caruso! Will they not be disappointed? They are not. They insist that it is the greatest thing they ever heard. . . ."

He was unwilling to join a group, headed by Reinhold Niebuhr and Bertolt Brecht, that proposed forming a "Free-German" government in exile and declined, in May 1944, to sign a manifesto of the "Council for Democratic Germany." The invasion of Europe (on June 6, 1944, his sixty-ninth birthday), the prospect of a German collapse, and the emerging plans for *Doctor Faustus*, a novel with a broad view of contemporary European culture suggested an article on "What is German?," which was further developed in an address given in May, 1945, at the Library of Congress, entitled "Germany and the Germans."

In June 1944 he became an American citizen; he continued his BBC talks to Germany and actively supported the re-election of Roosevelt, at whose death in April 1945 he delivered a memorial eulogy in Santa Monica. With almost single-minded concentration he worked on the *Faustus*-novel. His seventieth birthday, one month after the capitulation of Nazi Germany, was the occasion for a splendid testimonial dinner in New York, at which Robert Sherwood presided and Justice Frankfurter and Harold Ickes were the chief speakers. He rejected the suggestion that he might now return to Germany, but was delighted that some of his works were soon to be available again to his German readers. Work on *Faustus* was interrupted in May 1946 by a most serious lung operation in Chicago, from which he slowly recovered. He returned at once to *Faustus*: after three years and eight months of sustained involvement this, his most ambitious novel, was completed in January 1947. When it appeared later that year, it proved to be not only strikingly successful (like *Joseph the Provider* and later, *The Holy Sinner*, it was a Book-of-the-Month Club selection), but an achievement that deeply moved his readers in America and Europe.

His first trip to Europe after the war, in the summer of 1947, involved Mann in a series of political controversies: in an interview he seemed to accuse the Germans of self-pity and did not visit Germany, reason enough, so it seemed, for pointed attacks in the German press. After his return to California, he maintained, in lectures and interviews, a critical view of post-war Germany and, from time to time, voiced his concern over the Allied policy of creating a divided nation. Nietzsche and Goethe preoccupied him; an account of the years devoted to the writing of *Doctor Faustus* was completed in October 1948, and plans for two new novels began to take shape.

In July 1949, during the bicentennial year of Goethe's birth, Mann returned to Germany after an absence of sixteen years. "My heart," he said in "A Message to the Germans," "has remained with Germany; I, too, have suffered at the German fate. As an American citizen I have remained a German writer, faithful to the German language which I consider my true native realm." In Frankfurt he delivered an impressive Goethe lecture which he agreed to repeat in East Germany; Weimar as well as Frankfurt awarded him the Goethe Prize. His decision to speak in the East was as resolute as it turned out to be politically disturbing: it was resented no less in West Germany than in the United States, and appeared to imply sympathy for a political philosophy unacceptable to both.

When in April 1950 Mann felt obliged to cancel a lecture, "The Years of My Life," at the Library of Congress, he did so because he feared the protests of those who would accuse him of "communist" sympathies. Such political insinuations continued to trouble him throughout that year and the next. While he stubbornly pursued work on two novels, *The Holy Sinner* and *Felix Krull*, he defended himself against suggestions of "pro-communist" sentiments. In April and June 1951, he explicitly rejected these hysterical accusations and warned publicly against the increasingly ominous persecution of political dissidents in the United States. In November 1951 he was elected to the Academy of Arts and Letters, an event that filled him with pride: "America has just received me . . . with much publicity among its fifty immortals" as "a creative artist whose works are likely to achieve a permanent place in the Nation's culture."

Yet, his stays in Europe during the summer of 1950 and, especially, 1951 had strengthened his feeling that he should permanently return there. In June 1952 he left the United States for the last time, to settle for the remaining three years of his life in Switzerland. As he looked back on more than a decade of exile, he spoke with profound gratitude. But, he concluded, "it is a fact that the longer I lived there, the more I became conscious of my being a European. Despite the most comfortable living conditions, I felt, especially at my advanced age, ever more urgently, an almost anxious wish to return home to that native earth in which I hope one day to come to rest."

If Mann thought of the years in America as years of exile, they were far different in their altogether generous cast, their scope for sustained work, and their public effectiveness from the life of deprivation which most of his fellow refugees were compelled to live. Talent and circumstances permitted him to act as spokesman for a liberal tradition that seemed itself the very cause for which the war was fought. This role he played demonstratively as a German who was content to remain, in language, manner, and conviction, almost untouched by the realities of an American way of life; it was this conscious detachment as much as his representative presence that enabled him to produce in America some of his most moving works as a German novelist.

The Mann Family

STANLEY CORNGOLD

The Mann family belongs to the history of literature for at least two generations. The brothers Heinrich (1871-1950) and Thomas (1875-1955) were immensely prolific writers throughout their long lifetimes. Thomas Mann and Katia Pringsheim Mann had six children, all of whom have published books; and a number of the works of the late Klaus Mann (1906-1949), a novelist and essayist, and Golo Mann (b. 1909), a historian, are of considerable importance. With a little imagination one could include in this "writingest" of families even the mother of Thomas Mann, Julia *née* da Silva-Bruhns, who composed a book of reminiscences and who introduced into the solidly burgher Mann family a specifically artistic sensibility. Nor should one overlook the memoirs of Thomas Mann's much younger brother Viktor (1890-1949)—*We Were Five*. But Viktor, a bank official, was without serious literary aspirations.

The mother of Heinrich and Thomas Mann, a forceful woman of German, Brazilian, and Creole descent, had been brought to Germany as a child. She exerted by all accounts a powerful formative influence on both Heinrich and Thomas, exciting their love of the fabulous and the exotic and, not unimportantly, supervising their musical education. A number of Thomas Mann's works have indeed fabulous settings. The Joseph tetralogy takes place in ancient Egypt, *The Transposed Heads*, in India; but more important is the fact that all of Thomas Mann's novels are to some extent reflections on the exotic. They turn on the intrusion into conventional modes of a wholly different spirit or personality or style of life—something forbidden, dissolving, remissive. It was no small thing for the young man, growing up in the sedate Hanseatic city of Lübeck, to realize that through his father's marriage this very exoticism flowed in his veins, was not only a speculative possibility of his nature but literally part of his constitution. If Mann's works are modern, this is due much less to their technical innovations than to their intense perception of an omnipresent demon of disorder.

Meanwhile the importance of Mann's musical education can

be seen very obviously in his work: in the force with which his prose "aspires to the condition of music," notwithstanding its often worldly, plainly realistic content; in his essays on Schopenhauer and Wagner; and in the great prominence of music in his "wildest book," *Doctor Faustus.*

But the figure having the greatest influence on Thomas Mann during his first years as a writer was another family member—his brother Heinrich. Heinrich showed Thomas the way to the vocation of writing: he enjoyed an absolute superiority over his younger brother while both were adolescents. It was Heinrich who preceded Thomas to the old Katharineum College in Lübeck; who introduced him to the "daring" writers: Heine, Nietzsche, the psychological novelist Paul Bourget; and who showed at first the more obvious artistic talent, both literally as a painter and then by the exuberance of his literary imagination. And so it was Heinrich who, unlike Thomas, could write serenely that his brother hadn't "disturbed him a bit." But was this a stance which Heinrich could long have maintained? After the great success of Thomas' *Buddenbrooks* (1901), and on account of the immense disparity in their work and life style, Thomas must surely have disturbed his brother profoundly.

The astonishing success of *Buddenbrooks* must have been a most trying fact of life for Heinrich to assimilate, for he had in a sense presided over its writing. Shortly after the death of their father, Senator Johann Heinrich Mann, Thomas and Heinrich travelled to Italy on modest legacies. There they remained from 1896 to 1898, sharing rooms in various cheap pensions and, especially in Palestrina and Rome, writing continuously. Heinrich wrote novellas and began work on a major novel, *Im Schlaraffenland (In Cloudcuckooland)*; Thomas began writing his first sketches for *Buddenbrooks.* (Thomas had begun negotiating a volume of short stories with the Samuel Fischer publishing house of Berlin; now in response to Fischer's request for something a bit longer, "perhaps a novel," Thomas was embarking on a long work indeed, a novel in two thick volumes!) So intimate was the connection between the brothers at this time that they could briefly contemplate composing *Buddenbrooks* as a joint project.

In Italy the brothers read their work to each other. Here is early evidence for the impression one has from their novels that each is alert to the content of the other's work, and each, in his own fiction, alludes deliberately to his brother's literary personas. Thomas Mann's American biographer, Richard Winston, has recently spoken of this fictional inscription of the Manns' awareness of being brothers.* Thomas' novels continually feature brother-pairs or virtual brother-pairs (in *Tonio Kröger*, for example, there is Tonio and Hans; in *The Magic Mountain*, Hans and Joachim; in *Doctor Faustus*, Serenus and Adrian). Specific allusions can become quite cruel. Heinrich's essay on Zola (1915) alludes scathingly to a prematurely successful career like that of brother Thomas, doomed to "dry him out" early. Meanwhile, the figure of Settembrini in *The Magic Mountain* patently incorporates less attractive features of Heinrich: his garrulousness, his facility, even the shabbiness of his dress.

The plain fact was that in 1905, the year of his marriage, Thomas was a wealthy social and literary success, and Heinrich none of these things. Heinrich strove with unflagging energy for a comparable recognition; by 1909 he had written ten novels and countless short stories to Thomas' two novels and two thin volumes of short stories. Thomas could grow mortified at the example that such activity set him; his whole life he feared the charge of "laziness" (!), and he at once dreaded but could not completely avoid his "worst hours" in which he felt hatred of his brother. In the years of the first world war, however, the difference between them was to grow implacable, as Germany's situation drew from the brothers opposite and extreme responses.

For Thomas this war, or Germany's "defensive struggle," was profoundly justified; for Heinrich, a horrible waste. Thomas saw the war as a conflict not of nations but of principles in which Germany took up arms on behalf of embattled *Kultur* against English and French "civilization"—a shallow affair of technology and "enlightenment" in the service of the profit motive. Thomas contrived a position out of scraps of Nietzsche and Wagner and patriotic historians, one that in the end would not offend by one iota the German majority war party. This compendium of trials and errors in conservative poses is his outrageous, brilliant, and muddled book—*Reflections of a Non-Political Man* (1918). Thomas wrote all during the war on behalf of the German homeland—the "deeper, darker, hotter world" of native values; Heinrich found this unpolitical extremism abhorrent. His response was a famous essay on Zola in defense of intellectuality and its implicit commitment to action. This

* "Being Brothers—Thomas and Heinrich Mann," an address delivered at Rutgers University on April 12, 1975. My own remarks are indebted to Mr. Winston's paper.

"exchange" of works marks the low point of sympathy between the brothers. Their relation for several years after the war was shaped entirely by political passion. Thomas wrote in 1918: "Let the tragedy of our brotherhood unfold."

They were to come together again; Thomas' advocacy, however grudging, of the German Republic closed the distance between their views. Their relations from this point on are marked by a return to a common sanity and common cares after the ascendancy of the Nazis. Their speedily expressed revulsion at this regime—and their later exile together in America—helped them to find, often, a common ground of political and moral beliefs. Key differences remained, which the following parallel illustrates. In spring 1950, Heinrich's fatal illness cut short a decade of Communist activity and frustrated his intention to emigrate to East Germany. At the same time, Thomas would cancel a talk before the Library of Congress, fearing to provoke the charge of "fellow traveler." But now as ever, since their reconciliation in 1922, Thomas did not fail to praise in writing the fundamental integrity of his brother's life and work. In 1951, Professor Alfred Kantorowicz wrote Mann of the ceremonies which the (East) German Academy of Arts contemplated in honor of the eightieth anniversary of the birth of Heinrich Mann. Thomas replied (in a letter in the possession of the Princeton University Library, dated March 16, 1951):

> These ceremonies can contribute to disseminating among the German people . . . the knowledge of what a treasure it possesses in the dauntless life's work of this spirit—nobly solitary and, for all that, passionately dedicated to democracy—a spirit full of the proud impulse toward beauty and social vision who in all the brilliance of his artistic gifts wanted nothing more than to serve, to better, to help, to show the way toward goodness. Gratitude came late to him; for the Germans, the combination of the literary artist with the political moralist was too strange a thing for his critical genius to have been able to change their destiny; and even today I fear that few of them know that this dead man was one of their greatest writers. May your celebration be a sign that, now that he has gone out of time, his time has come.

The children of Thomas and Katia Mann were born to them in pairs. The first-born, Erika (1905-1969) and Klaus (1906-1949), lived active, adventurous, and productive lives, but in Klaus' case creativity exacted a harsh price: his life ended in suicide a month after the death of Viktor Mann.

Of all the Mann children, Erika was much the closest to her

father. This point is ironical. Thomas announced her birth to Heinrich as follows: "It's a girl: a disappointment to me, I admit, . . . for I had very much wanted a boy and haven't stopped wanting one. . . . Perhaps my daughter will bring me into an inwardly closer relation to the 'opposite' sex which, even though I am now a married man, I really still don't know a thing about." Ultimately, Mann was to care a good deal more for his three daughters than for his three sons.

His intimacy with Erika extended even to the inner sanctum of his creative work. From 1945 on, Erika was an invaluable co-worker and editor. On October 26, 1946, Mann wrote her à propos of *Doctor Faustus* of "our slenderized little book." Erika had proposed various cuts which Mann had, happily, agreed to. She also scrutinized the manuscript of *Felix Krull* for inconsistencies and suggested a number of changes. Mann addressed her in her inscription copy as "Eri, to whose keenness I owe many things in this book." After her father's death Erika edited a three-volume selection from his immense correspondence.

In her own right Erika won considerable fame as an actress, lecturer, and writer of great wit and resourcefulness. Her first choice of profession was the stage. She played classic roles (e.g. Jessica in *The Merchant of Venice*) in important theaters in Berlin and Hamburg. In 1925 Klaus Mann's play *Anja and Esther* was successfully premiered in Hamburg. The four key roles were filled by Klaus, Erika, Gustaf Gründgens (the great actor and director) and Pamela Wedekind (daughter of the Expressionist playwright). Subsequently Erika married Gründgens, but the marriage soon ended in divorce.

Erika gave up her stage career in 1930 to devote her energies as novelist, journalist, and cabarettist mainly to protest the detested Nazi regime. Competing in an automobile race with Klaus Mann she drove frantically up and down Europe from Helsinki to Venice, as if they had subliminally realized the truth of their coming displacement. By 1933 they had grasped, long before their father, the impossibility of life in Germany and warned him against returning home. And though the family house in Munich had already been confiscated by the Nazis, Erika bravely slipped back and rescued the completed manuscript of the first and second volume and the beginning of the third volume of the Joseph novels.

The achievement for which Erika won the greatest recognition was her cabaret "The Peppermill," which she staged in Munich in 1933 and then, under pressure of Nazi threats, resettled in Zurich; the theater enjoyed an immense success. It inspired her father to write her of the "forever increasing admiration and love" he felt for her. From her attempt to transplant the cabaret to America arose her activity as lecturer, and once, in 1942, she made a tour of fifty cities. She wrote a number of books during this period, including a major study of the Nazi education of children, *School for Barbarians* (1938), and, with Klaus, a memoir, *Escape to Life* (1939).

Erika spent most of the war years in an activity suited to her daring and combative nature—as a correspondent in various theaters of war. From 1945 on, a good deal of her energy went into cooperation with her father and the writing of books and films serving the accurate commemoration and interpretation of his achievement. One detail of her personal life offers a curious hint of that coming together of European élite which her father greatly advocated—a union that in many cases could not become reality without the crass intervention of the Nazi disaster. With W. H. Auden she contracted in 1936 a *mariage de convenance*.

Klaus, of all the Mann children, was, in his short lifetime, most wholeheartedly a writer. At eighteen he had already published stories and theater criticism, and a year later his first two books appeared—a volume of short fiction called *Vor dem Leben (Before Life)* and a novel, *The Pious Dance*. Despite his labile and troubled personality, he wrote conscientiously and prolifically. His schooling was erratic and his early years marked by the scandals of the *enfant terrible*. Thomas Mann's story "Disorder and Early Sorrow" communicates something of his parents' concern for his divagations during years of social turmoil. In the 1920s Klaus was a successful playwright and actor. In 1928 he travelled to the United States and with his sister—he wrote in an autobiographical sketch—"delivered lectures on modern German literature to various universities such as Harvard and Princeton." The product of this trip was the novel *Adventure*.

The turning point in his life was Hitler's coming to power: Klaus left Germany in 1933. For three years, in Amsterdam, he edited the important émigré literary journal *Die Sammlung*. In 1936 he came to America, where he founded another anti-fascist "magazine of free culture," *Decision*, lectured frequently, and wrote a number of novels and memoirs of which *The Turning Point* (1942) and its posthumously published German version,

Der Wendepunkt (1952), are the most important. This work, an autobiographical account of his struggle for a coherent life, is organized around a series of crises; it manipulates a variety of styles; its form dramatizes the difficulty of its theme. After America entered the war, Klaus Mann enlisted in the U.S. Army as a specialist in psychological warfare. He spent his last years in the south of France, subject to severe depression, which he described lucidly in several essays. He committed suicide in 1949.

Golo (b. 1909) and Monika (b. 1910) are the middle pair of Mann children. Golo is today a renowned historian. He wrote a doctoral dissertation at Heidelberg on "the concept of the individual in Hegel" and shortly thereafter, in 1933, emigrated to France. He taught German history as an assistant professor at the University of Rennes and contributed numerous articles on political and historical subjects to the émigré journal *Mass und Wert*.

After volunteering for war duty in France as an ambulance driver, he was interned but managed to escape and, after harrowing adventures, arrived in America. Like his brother Klaus, he enlisted in Army Intelligence. He stayed in Germany after the war as a civil administrator but sought eagerly to return to the United States to resume his academic career. He has been Professor of History at Claremont College and thereafter at the University of Münster and the Stuttgart Polytechnic. Golo's historical scholarship is vast; he has published several prize-winning works. His history of Germany in the nineteenth and twentieth centuries is familiar to English and American readers in a Penguin edition. He has recently been celebrated for a long narrative of the life of Wallenstein.

His sister Monika writes fiction. Like her brother Michael she has been trained as a musician, and like many members of her family she has published a memoir. But unlike the rest of her family, she suffered a shattering personal blow as a direct consequence of the war. In 1939 she married a young Hungarian art historian, Jenö Lányi. The following year both set sail for Canada on the freighter "City of Benares." The ship was torpedoed by a German U-boat. Her husband drowned; she clung to the rim of a bottomless lifeboat in rough seas for twenty hours until she was rescued by an English warship. A good deal of her life has been spent in the effort to come to terms with this calamity.

Elisabeth Mann-Borgese was born in 1918, her brother Michael a year later. At twenty, Elisabeth married the brilliant scholar and political activist Giuseppe Borgese, thirty-seven years her senior. Together at the University of Chicago they edited the journal *Common Cause*. She is the author of novels, of a constitution for a world government, and of books and articles of social importance, notably the women's liberationist work, *Ascent of Woman*.

Michael Mann is an accomplished violinist and violist and is Professor of German at the University of California at Berkeley. He is a productive scholar and has published important articles on his father's work as well as books on Goethe, Schiller, and the history of music.

It is almost impertinent in such a brief compass to attempt to do justice to Thomas Mann's widow Katia, who, at ninety-two, lives today, fit and lucid, in Küsnacht near Zurich. Her marriage to Thomas Mann was an unusually happy and affectionate one, despite the turmoil of emigration and the suicide of her eldest son.* A passage from a letter which Mann wrote to Hans Riesiger (June 30, 1950) begins to suggest her importance to him. Shortly after Mann's seventy-fifth birthday, Katia Mann had had to spend several weeks in a Swiss hospital. Mann wrote: "As splendid a daughter as Erika is, I still feel lonely, nervous, without my accustomed protection: I am unable to pursue my work. . . ."

* The reader curious for details may now consult Katia Mann's *Unwritten Memoirs*, published just this year in New York.

PHOTOGRAPHIC CREDITS

All photographs are from the Caroline Newton Collection of Thomas Mann. The photographer on pages 27, 30, 31, and 34 is unknown.

28. Katia Mann: Fr. Müller
28. Mann and daughter: E. Wasow
29. Thomas Mann: Vaněk
33. Thomas Mann: Thea Goldmann
33. Mann and wife: Florence Homolka